Testimonials

"In rapidly evolving markets, CPAs must change how they operate. While we guide our clients to adapt and grow, Bridget reminds us that transformation must begin from within. She delivers an insightful and engaging roadmap for building proactive, efficient, and sustainable CPA firms that meet the demand of modern advisory services. Her story is fun, inspiring, and educational, offering essential guidance for CPAs supporting Main Street."

Thomas Jasiak, CPA, CVA
Thomas Jasiak CPA, LLC

"*Upskill or Out* made me feel like I was walking in Bridget's shoes. As a fellow business owner, I felt seen by her honest reflections on the pressure to serve clients well while trying to build something more sustainable and maintain personal balance. Bridget turns her hard-won experience into a practical framework others can actually use, showing that AI is not just about efficiency; it is about creating capacity, delivering more value, and building something better for your business, your clients, and yourself. A timely read for leaders ready to rethink how they work, serve, and grow."

Leslie Vickrey
CEO & Founder, ClearEdge

"While working in a large health system and not as a small business owner, I found this book's message incredibly practical and relevant. It offers a thoughtful and approachable perspective on how AI can augment human thinking, reduce the burden of everyday work, and help professionals reclaim time for family, purpose, and the parts of life that matter most. A smart and relatable read for anyone looking to work smarter, not harder."

Jill A. Graziano, RN, BSN, MBA
President & COO, Unity Hospital and
United Memorial Medical Center

"Success in business often depends on staying focused on the big picture while navigating an endless stream of small but overwhelming details. *Upskill or Out* offers a practical, approachable guide to accepting and utilizing AI as a powerful business partner. More than anything, it shows how AI can give back something every business owner needs more of — focus and time."

Dan Johnson
VP of Operations
Technicraft Manufacturing Inc.

"Implementing AI into our business over the past eight months has dramatically improved our efficiency, communication, and project organization. The systems and operational improvements Bridget introduced, which are reflected in the principles of *Upskill or Out,* have become a major competitive advantage and time-saver for our business."

Brian Hume
President, Backwoods Custom, Inc.

UPSKILL OR OUT

AI, Small Business,
and the New American Dream

BRIDGET WAY, CPA

Published by Rethink Books, Charleston, South Carolina.
An imprint of Advantage Media.

Rethink Books colophon is a trademark of Advantage Media.
Printed in the United States of America.

10 9 8 7 6 5 4 3 2 1

ISBN: 979-8-90389-011-8 (Paperback)

Cover design by AZ Herrera.
Layout design by Ronald Pono.

Rethink Books is an imprint of Advantage Media Group. Advantage Media helps busy entrepreneurs, CEOs, and leaders write and publish a book to grow their business and become the authority in their field. Rethink Books authors comprise a community of industry professionals, idea-makers, and thought leaders. For more information go to books.rethinkpress.com.

CONTENTS

ACKNOWLEDGEMENT

This book would not have been possible without the people who supported me and encouraged me to bring this idea to life.

I am forever grateful to my family for their unwavering support throughout this journey. To my husband and children, thank you for your patience, love, and support throughout this process. Writing a book takes time, focus, and energy, and I know that some of that came at the expense of moments with you. Thank you for giving me the opportunity to write, think, and chase this dream I have had for years. Your support made this book possible, and I love you all so much. Thank you for standing by me every step of the way.

To my parents, thank you for your continued love, support, and belief in me. Your encouragement throughout my life has created the foundation of who I am today and made this process possible. I am grateful for the values you instilled in me, the confidence you helped build, and always being there to support me.

A special thank you to my dear friend Leslie Vickrey, who inspired me to write this book and helped me take the first steps toward making it happen. Your encouragement and guidance in getting connected with my publisher gave this project momentum when it was still just an idea.

Heartfelt thanks to all my friends who checked in, cheered me on, and reminded me why I took on this endeavor in the first place. Your support meant more than you know.

To my clients, thank you for trusting me to guide you on your financial journeys. Your businesses, challenges, and dreams are at the heart of this book. You have allowed me to grow not only as a CPA, but as an advisor, problem solver, and partner in your pursuit of stability and success.

I would also like to acknowledge Zack Kass and Pascal Finette, whose work and perspectives on artificial intelligence, disruption, innovation, and the changing world around us have inspired me. Their ideas helped shape the way I think about the future of work, the profession I serve, and the importance of staying curious and open to change.

Finally, to the readers who pick up this book, thank you. My hope is that these pages encourage you to see AI not as something to fear, but as a tool to help you reclaim time, restore balance, and continue building your own version of the American Dream.

FOREWORD

Accountants are creatures of habit. I say that with affection and complete self-awareness, because I am one of them. We learn our systems, trust what has worked, and hang on tightly to the routines that carried us through one deadline after another. In our world, familiarity can feel like security. We use the same language, rely on the same references, and often cling to the same methods long after the profession has started moving in a different direction.

As an industry, there is no doubt that we are losing good people to exhaustion, stress, and existential dread. When I first met Bridget, it was at a memorial of sorts. We connected because our local CPA community had recently lost two of our top professionals, and it felt like the right time to come together and support each other in whatever way we could.

Naturally, when Bridget mentioned that she was embracing AI in her practice, I had a hard time hiding my eye rolls. But when she doubled down and said she was writing a book about it, I decided to give it a chance.

During my career, I have been far from an early adopter. In fact, I consider myself someone who resists change until change practically drags me into the room. When I first began hearing people talk about artificial intelligence, especially in accounting, I did not feel excitement. I felt suspicion and the overwhelming thought of having to learn a new language. And, as I suspect many folks with linear, math-oriented brains like my own, learning a new language never goes well. Just ask my high school Spanish teacher and my Duolingo app.

When I started reading *Upskill or Out*, it felt like the floodgates opened. Because the author is a CPA and small business expert, this book comes from the ground up, not from a 30,000-foot aerial view. The chapters approach topics through practical steps, not theoretical ramblings.

That is why this book clarified my perspective in such a meaningful way. It did not convince me by making AI sound flashy, futuristic, or inevitable. It changed my mind because it made the subject practical, human, and relevant to the real lives of accountants and small business owners. Bridget does not write from a distance. She writes as someone who has lived the long tax seasons, the messy books, the endless follow-up emails, and the weight of being the person clients depend on when they are confused, worried, or behind. That matters. It means readers are not getting a theory of the future. They are getting the hard-earned perspective of someone who understands exactly what the old way costs.

What became clear to me as I read these chapters is that *Upskill or Out* is not really a book about choosing technology for technology's sake. It is a book about choosing a better way to work. Bridget describes a profession and a business model that many of us recognize immediately: reactive, deadline-driven, and dependent on a level of sustained exhaustion that too many accountants accept as normal. She also calls out an important concept that all professionals need to hear: burnout is not a badge of honor, and survival is not the same thing as success.

That perspective shift was important for me. Bridget shows that AI, used well, is not about replacing judgment, experience, or relationships. It is about removing repetitive friction so that professionals can spend more time doing the work that actually requires discernment and care. The value of AI is not speed for its own sake. The value is what that speed makes possible: cleaner books, better systems, stronger advisory relationships, and more room for thoughtful decision-making.

The book clarifies something larger than workflow. It shows that this conversation is not just about accountants trying to keep up with software, because technology cannot replicate trust. It cannot replace the relationship between an advisor and a client, especially in small communities where business is personal and reputations are built over time. Instead, Bridget argues that the right tools can protect and even deepen those relationships by freeing professionals from unnecessary manual work and allowing them to show up with greater clarity and value.

I also appreciated that this book did not ask me to abandon skepticism altogether. In fact, part of what makes it persuasive is that it does not present blind enthusiasm as wisdom. Bridget acknowledges the emotional resistance, the risks of poor implementation, the importance of trust, and the need for human oversight. She does not suggest that every shiny new tool deserves our loyalty. She argues for intention, discernment, and practical application. Bridget understands not only the promise of AI, but also the hesitation many of us feel when confronted with one more change in an already demanding profession.

By the time I finished reading, my perspective was much clearer. I no longer saw this as a conversation about whether accountants and small business owners should surrender to a trend. I saw it as a conversation about whether we are willing to let go of needless suffering when better tools are available. I saw that adapting does not mean losing the parts of the profession that matter most. If anything, it protects them. It means preserving expertise, relationships, and the capacity to serve people well without sacrificing every ounce of energy in the process.

That is why this book matters. It speaks to professionals who are tired of the old grind but wary of empty promises. It offers not hype, but clarity. Not abstraction, but application. And for readers like me, who may approach the subject with folded arms and raised eyebrows, it offers something even more valuable: a new perspective grounded in experience, honesty, and hope.

Michele Knight, CPA

PREFACE

If you have ever sat alone in the quiet hours, feeling like your business is swallowing you whole and wondering how you can keep going, this book is for you.

For nearly two decades, I have run a small CPA firm in a mountain town, and for years, I followed the typical model of small CPA public accounting firms. My workload was very heavy from January through April. I was inundated. I carried mountains of information in my head, constantly trying to carve order out of chaos. Behind every return and every spreadsheet was a person who was tired, anxious, and trying their best.

The long hours, often at the expense of time away from my family, and the emotional toll of trying to keep everyone "financially relevant," began weighing heavily. I often would take on one more client and fix the accounting software mess just in time for the tax deadline.

My clients are not Fortune 500 companies. They are middle class working people like me. They are coffee shop owners, contractors I have known for 20+ years, mercantile owners run by a family to ensure the locals and the tourists have all their basic needs. To most of them, I'm "Bridget, the accountant, not "Bridget, the professional service firm." They call me when they get a letter in the mail from the IRS, when they have a quick accounting question, or whether they can hire their child to work for the family business.

Over time, I began to realize that I had so much more to offer them than transactional accounting. Many of my clients are my friends, and I care deeply for them and their families. It was time I started walking alongside them as a trusted advisor and not just work on clean up and tax preparation once a year.

I didn't set out to write a book about artificial intelligence. I was inspired by a group of women to share my story and inspire business owners that working long hours does not need to define your success. Although I am a CPA and write from the perspective of an accountant, the content is geared and relevant to small business owners.

This book is the story of how I found a better way. It is not a love letter to technology. It's a guide from a small-town CPA who was determined to keep doing the work I loved. I became an accountant because I loved problem solving, and accounting was a math problem that could be solved.

My grandfather was an Enrolled Agent when I was growing up in the 1980's and 1990's, back when accounting looked very different. There were no dashboards or cloud-based software. No instant recalculations, which meant every change meant starting over. He would use a typewriter to enter the numbers legibly on a paper copy that you would pick up from the local library.

I witnessed and heard stories of how my grandfather operated his business. He built a successful practice. He was respected, trusted, and loved by his clients. I didn't fully understand what that meant until his funeral.

The number of clients and flowers presented was overwhelming to me at the age of nineteen. These were people he had helped for decades. People whose businesses he had helped prosper even in moments of financial uncertainty. They didn't just respect him; they adored him.

But success came at a cost. My dad tells stories about how he and his brother would be awoken from a deep sleep, one, two in the morning. They would hear him yelling obscenities at himself for making an error. He would berate himself for even the smallest error, knowing that fixing the error may mean retyping the entire return. There was no undo button.

My father and his siblings saw that life and wanted no part of it. They grew up with the sound of frustration echoing through the house throughout the day from January through April. My sister started studying accounting in college, but it never became her thing. And yet, somehow, I was inspired.

I knew the demands of the profession. But I loved numbers, and I was good with them. I loved the idea of helping people make sense of their finances. I didn't see accounting as a punishment. I saw it as a math problem that I could solve. As a career, I saw it as a purpose and a way I could have flexibility and support my family.

Even at the beginning of my career, I learned from my grandfather's ways. I set clear guidelines and deadlines. My grandfather gave everything to his clients. The tools of his time demanded his nights, his rest, and often his peace. People of that era saw no other way. Today, there is another way.

AI doesn't diminish what was done in the past for accountants. I think it honors them in a way. It removes the stress that once consumed many brilliant minds in the field. Automation and AI support provide speed and safety. It allows us to service clients outside of compliance, without sacrificing ourselves in the process.

When I think about my grandfather, I don't wish he had worked less hard. I wish he had better tools. The new American Dream doesn't ask us to suffer to prove our worth. By using the tools of today, we can build wisely, live fully, and protect both ourselves and our clients.

OVERVIEW

Accounting has always been the backbone of American small business. Yet for decades, accountants and entrepreneurs alike have been trapped in a cycle of long nights, envelopes of receipts, paper copies, spreadsheets, software files, and continuous financial chaos.

I didn't start out in this business for the love of the grind. I became an accountant because I loved numbers, and they made sense to me, and I liked using analytics to solve problems. Somewhere along the way the joy got buried under the workload, but it was there once, and it mattered.

The work really took a toll on me during and after COVID. The long hours. The constant pressure to "get it right," despite incomplete guidance from the government or missing information from clients. The feeling that my knowledge, education, and experience were being used to put out fires instead of to prevent them. There were many days I wondered, "Is this really what I signed up for?"

Transactional accounting had run its course in my business. I knew deep down I had more to offer. I wanted to be an advisor, a sounding board, someone who could help clients grow, not just survive. I wanted to do tax planning before year-end, to understand their business. It turns out that I didn't like surprises any more than my clients did.

Then the world shifted. COVID did not invent uncertainty; it magnified it. Government programs and tax-law changes arrived faster than anyone could keep pace with. My phone rang constantly, people asking if they qualified for PPP relief, how to handle unemployment income, or what deductions they were entitled to with everything in their life changing. I was in the trenches with them and had to navigate the path to the best of my ability. There was no playbook on how to handle this.

The panic over decisions that could shape their financial future became personal, because I cared and I, too, was afraid.

The fear felt personal. It was at this time that I realized I needed to make a change to my business. Not only for me, but for my clients as well. There had to be a better way.

At first, I thought this change meant working differently. How could I address the long hours and the endless research to provide insight to each new nuance that was introduced as a result of the shutdown? Software and technology became essential at this point. I needed to be as efficient as possible and provide accurate information. Small businesses now could compete with large corporations, as software was designed to be cost effective to them as well. Artificial intelligence was quite new, but it was in the background, with blockchain as one example.

The rise of artificial intelligence is not just changing how firms and small businesses keep their books; it's reshaping what it means to work, live, and pursue the American Dream.

In *Upskill or Out*, I share my journey from QuickBooks Desktop "warrior" to AI-powered advisor through vivid stories, like my spreadsheet client who sent unreconciled last-minute files, or my paper bag client who faithfully brought monthly receipts. I will show that AI doesn't replace accountants or small business owners; it strengthens their ability to turn unsystematic records into clear financial data and stops the cycle of reactive bookkeeping. Focusing on having clean data creates less busy work, which in return allows us to focus on relationships, good decision making, and the steady work of building healthy businesses and balanced lives.

Blending storytelling, practical frameworks, and a hopeful vision for the future, this book is both a guide and an inspiration. It demonstrates that technology supports small businesses, enabling them to prosper without losing human touch.

Most of us who build small businesses are chasing the American Dream. My inspiration for my business was to have something of my own that offered flexibility and financial security.

My hope is that by the end of the book, you will understand what AI can do for your business, and that you will feel empowered to use it. Do not fear AI. Look at it as your sidekick or personal assistant. It is not intended to replace you, but to elevate the work you have spent so much time building. It is just a tool as a hammer is to a contractor. Use this tool to eliminate the mundane boring tasks and elevate your skills in other areas to provide value and confidence to keep moving to the American Dream you envision.

The American Dream was never meant to be a life of constant urgency or missed moments. It was meant to offer opportunities, freedom, and economic security. And for me, starting my own business was my way of obtaining my dream.

The world is evolving at a fast pace. Working harder is not the answer, but working on elevating your growth and upskilling your knowledge in today's environment will put you in a position for success.

CHAPTER 1

The Old Ledger

I WAS A QUICKBOOKS DESKTOP WARRIOR

STARTING IN JANUARY, I would be glued to my computer, and the work felt daunting right out of the gates. Software files were open on multiple screens, and I spent my days diving into company files, reconciling accounts, and making the kinds of adjustments that clients never saw but that made all the difference to preparing their tax returns. This was typical practice in small accounting firms, to be performing compliance accounting to complete their tax returns in the early 2000's era. It focuses on correct transaction classification, complete documentation, and timely payments. However, it is generally very reactive. This model of annual tax filing, with no prior work throughout the year with the business records, often creates stress both to the firm and the clients.

People always imagine me drowning in piles of paperwork and working until midnight into the tax deadlines. The truth is that the late-night marathon was never my thing. However, I did work relentless hours in comparison to a lot of other careers. I just chalked it up to, "Well, I signed up for this!"

The accounting software was the reason I could deliver and often the reason I stayed up late. It felt a bit like chasing a fix; you could never quite get enough of the data you needed. Even with the software, I still had to track down liability balances, invoices for big purchases, and other tax details that make or break a return.

All of this happened in a tiny window between January 1st and April 15th. What I usually got instead was random documents, half complete numbers, missing items, which required countless follow-ups trying to pull the data together into an accurate return. This felt so chaotic and was downright daunting and exhausting. The haphazard data being sent made me feel like a dog chasing its tail. I was a problem solver, and I wanted my clients' returns to be correct. The lack of consistency in tax documentation opened room for error.

THE SPREADSHEET AND THE PAPER BAG

One example of this was my spreadsheet client. Every March, she would send me her income and expenses on a spreadsheet with essentially no reconciliation of the data. She apologized for the last-minute data and hoped I had everything I needed to complete the tax return. There was always a need to ask for more information and data to support and provide a concise and accurate tax return, and this often came at the last minute.

The other client was a dear friend and operated a bit more old school. Everything came to me in a paper bag. I'd sort through the receipts and enter them into the software, one by one. Fortunately, this was not an annual ordeal. We had a monthly bookkeeping engagement to keep on the data regularly. Still, turning a bag of receipts into clean, usable financial data took time and added an extra layer of work to process.

Those two clients became the symbols of tax season for me. The spreadsheet and the paper bag. Every time I thought I'd seen issues in the software, they reminded me that there is often unpredictability in people's data, and chaos still found its way in.

TAX SEASON BECAME A DREADED ANNUAL RITUAL

The real test came in February and March. Software was supposed to make things efficient, but efficiency has its limits when dozens of clients all want their return filed yesterday. I'd be fixing year-long mistakes in their ledgers at 6 a.m., preparing tax returns by 9 a.m., and fielding phone calls throughout the day and into the evening hours.

It felt less like a busy season and more like a tax-season obstacle course: Constant reconciliations, balancing trial balances, and racing against deadlines that sprinted toward me like they had something to prove. Looking back, it is almost funny. At the time, I was just trying to stay caffeinated enough to keep the whole operation upright.

One night, I caught myself reclassifying the same transaction three times because I was too tired to notice I'd already fixed it. Another time, I filed a return only to realize later that income had been duplicated as they had undeposited funds, which had not been cleared up or handled properly in the cloud-based accounting system. This required an amendment and guilt on my part for missing this accounting error.

EMOTIONAL TOLL OF TAX SEASON CHAOS

I was worn down, but I respected my clients putting in long hours to fulfill their American Dream of owning a small business and being an entrepreneur. I could relate to their struggles, and they trusted me with their finances and businesses. And yet, as I helped them, I couldn't shake the feeling that my own dream of balance, freedom, and time with family was slipping further away each year. I missed countless dinners with my family and many events that my children were involved in during my busy season. I was proud of the work I did, but the personal cost was becoming harder to ignore.

FORESHADOWING THE COMING CHANGE

Long before I attended a technology conference or tested a piece of automation software, I could feel that change was coming.

The transformation was inevitable with agentic and generative AI. These platforms are no longer science fiction as we may have thought. They are rewriting how every industry works.

To thrive in this new landscape, I realized we need a new mindset. It is important that in accounting and small business, we facilitate a culture that promotes curiosity and learning AI skills so that the staff is in line with the changing trends of technology. The learning cannot be done on the side. It needs to be synchronized with the daily processes and tested and proven. Culture should promote learning, staying curious, and the willingness to experiment.

Looking forward is not optional in my opinion. It is the difference between leading and scrambling to keep up. AI isn't just another tool; it is a shift perhaps as profound as the Industrial Revolution. Moments like this reshape entire industries, and the people who thrive are the ones who choose to move early, learn fast, and stay curious.

Reactive work drains energy and creates burnout. Proactive thinking builds capacity, confidence, and opportunities. When change accelerates, waiting becomes a risky choice. Right now is the moment to lean in, experiment, and build the skills that will define the next era of work. We are not spectators in this transformation; we are participants. And the actions we take today will determine whether or not we are chasing the future or shaping it!

Change and uncertainty often feel intimidating. Growth comes from using what you know, building on it, and not fearing what you don't know. By focusing on your existing skills, you build confidence and momentum. In today's workplace, this is much like having equipment for the competition. An agile athlete faces challenges with adaptability and perseverance, leveraging the tools they need to succeed. Adopting this mindset empowers you to continually upskill and thrive in the evolving landscape of AI at work.

I didn't want to spend the next decade of my career reacting. I wanted to build a culture and systems that were ahead of the curve. Focusing on mindset, experimentation, and technology used with intention would become the partner I wanted to work with, and a team that supported that mindset. This quiet awareness, and the sense that something had to change before it broke me, was the whisper that eventually became impossible to ignore.

CHAPTER 2

The Whisper for Change

COVID WAS THE moment when uncertainty hit home, and I had reached my threshold. Sudden tax-law changes inundated clients. Every few days, guidance changed. Payroll updates, stimulus rules, and emergency funding all came faster than we could process. I was finding the process hard to navigate and support my clients. As a CPA, I watched people I cared about panic over decisions that could affect their financial future, and their fear felt personal. It was a difficult position to be in, trying to provide calm, clear guidance while facing the same unknowns, and I knew I had to change how I supported them. A single conviction came to me. I didn't need to prove my dedication through exhaustion.

THE CALL TO CHANGE

Every year after Tax Day, I always plan a trip with my family. This gives me something to look forward to while I am in the trenches of tax season. It was mid-April when my family and I broke away to the desert in Utah, away from laptops, internet, and cell service. The noise quieted in the crisp, spring air. There was no last-minute chaos or underlying stress in those moments. Obviously, this was not the answer, but there had to be a better way when I returned to my reality. That small, persistent idea set me on a path from QuickBooks specialist to a new kind of advisor. This moment became the seed of everything that followed.

A BETTER WAY

I didn't know yet what that better way looked like, only that hard work, software fixes, and tax compliance were no longer enough. Change was necessary. At first, "better" sounded like a fantasy. My entire profession revolved around deadlines, urgency, and crisis response.

I attended a conference where many classes promoted the idea of a hybrid service and not just bookkeeping and tax. I wanted to be more involved in the clients' businesses, so I was able to strategize with them to help them with taxes and other small business needs, such as analyzing their numbers to help them make shifts if necessary. I started jotting down ideas to create a better solution for my clients. Why not have a year-round accounting model where I acted as a true advisor and resolved problems as they came up rather than reactionary responses after the fact? I was sold on a proactive model approach, and I was going to make the shift.

CHANGE CULTURE, NOT JUST SYSTEMS

Culture in accounting is stubborn. I was taught by my grandfather that dedication and seventy-hour weeks were part of the job. January through April is inevitable misery, and that burnout is simply seasonal. However, his children did not follow suit in his career. Perhaps it was the late hours and constant stress that drove them away from this field?

I never liked that script but went into the profession as I was good with numbers, loved solving problems, and wanted to work for myself. I started to focus on sustainable workloads and mental health. I had a philosophy to do the work once and do it right. No rushing, no panic, but a workflow that had purpose and an end goal.

I encourage self-care to all staff members. Although I am generally operating solo, I often have part-time help throughout the year. I feel the emphasis on team building and partnership among all levels of staff need to be valued and acted upon. We live in a ski area. A few years back when I had a part-time staff member, we took a ski day together. We came back refreshed and rejuvenated after a recent deadline had just passed. I believe we were able to provide a better product for our clients in the end. I realize these were not radical innovations, but this was not something generally supported in my industry; I believed it was time for a change.

REIMAGINING THE RELATIONSHIP

Before COVID, my firm relationship with clients was defined by transactions. The clients would drop off their paperwork, I would prepare the return, review the return with them, and they would sign the documents. I would likely not see them again for a year. After changing to a proactive script in my firm, it shifted to participation. I was involved in their month-to-month earnings, cash flow challenges, and seasonality.

That small change altered everything. The numbers now had different meanings. They told a story of their hopes, dreams, and concerns. I could see when cash flow was tight and offer suggestions to lighten the load. The work transformed from compliance to a meaningful partnership with my clients. With a consistent connection comes trust and understanding.

THE NEW MODEL: CALM BY DESIGN

The "better way" finally started taking shape.

1. Predictable partnership: Clients had continuous monthly access to me, not frantic year-end calls.
2. Flat-rate pricing: They knew their costs upfront, which provided transparency and consistency.
3. Ongoing cleanup: Monthly reconciliations and review of data provided year-end readiness.

There was one mission. It became about redefining how to pursue the American Dream without burning out, for my clients and for myself. I designed a model that gives clients consistent monthly access to a trusted advisor and introduced flat-rate fees to eliminate last-minute tax-time shocks. We worked in tandem and learned and grew together to form habits that assisted the books to an elevated level beyond transactional accounting. It was important to educate the clients on the new system and its benefits. By shifting from reactive fixes to proactive planning, I built a firm culture that reduces surprises and helps clients pursue clearer, more sustainable financial goals. I wanted to eliminate surprises and panic after the year-end. I explained to clients why I was moving to this model.

The New Model

Calm by Design

A system designed to remove chaos from your financial life.

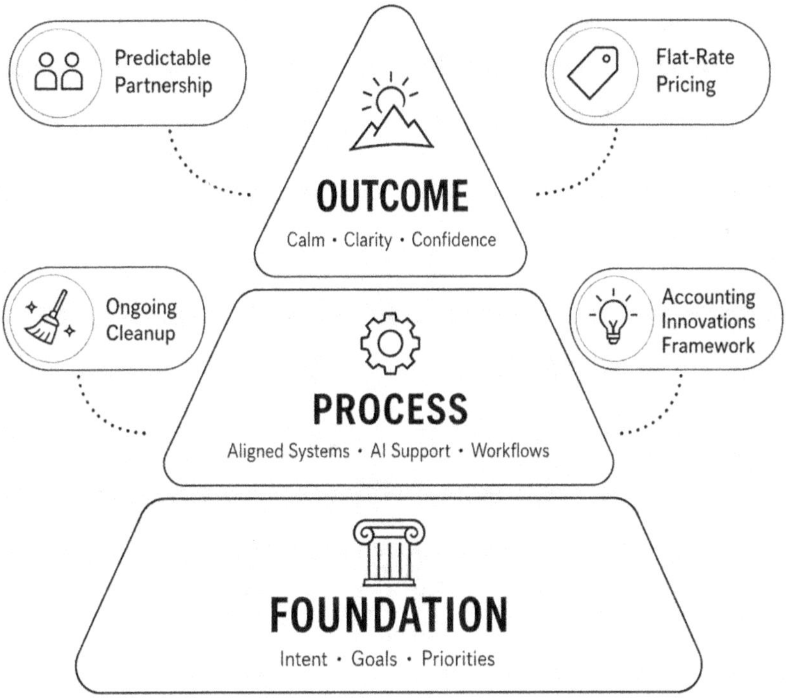

Calm isn't created by working harder.
It's designed through intention,
supported by systems, and sustained by the right tools.

SMALL WINS THAT BUILD CONFIDENCE

Positive habits rarely change just one thing. When I brought on a new communication tool in late 2021, I did get a bit of pushback from my clients. I received feedback from one client that they could not find a correspondence amongst the multiple threads. When I taught them that they could filter data by dates and tags, they saw that there was fluidity in the system, and it worked well. The how-to videos were very helpful in forming the habits needed in communicating my needs to get the data necessary to finish my processes. As their habits changed, data was uploaded regularly, and I noticed small wins and success using the tool.

I could set a task to remind clients to upload certain data in order to produce financial statements. Financial clarity can provide much needed peace to business owners. Small victories showed me that it was not only possible to stop chasing work but also to reshape it to make it more meaningful.

Could the "better way" also be smarter, faster, and more accurate? Could technology extend the balanced model I was building? I did not have these answers yet, but I was ready to find out.

THE HEART OF THE DECISION

Looking back, the pivot was driven by the chaos and the panic during the COVID shutdown. Reacting to every crisis felt unsustainable. In some ways, it misaligned with the level of guidance my clients deserved. I realized I needed to stop operating in a constant react and fix mode and instead help my clients build a stronger foundation. One that provided clarity and a long-term vision for their financial health.

I wanted to build advisory into my practice so that I could have a solid relationship with my clients. This drove my business and provided my purpose in moving forward as an accountant/CPA.

CHAOS TO COMPASS

The pandemic didn't invent my burnout. That was already a trend in the industry. However, the panic of the shutdown exposed the burn out. It turned down the noise just enough for me to hear the whisper that had been there for years: *There must be a better way.*

I didn't have a crystal ball. I didn't have a clear map of how the change would take shape. I just knew it was time for change. For me, my family, and my clients.

I was excited about being a proactive advisor. As I reimagined the firm, the whisper turned into direction and inspiration. I was redefining the way I worked with my clients. I knew this was just the beginning, but I had changed behaviors and expectations to allow for my clients to adapt with me as new changes continue to come. Changing the culture of my business was the answer.

CHAPTER 3

Enter Artificial Intelligence

CURIOSITY OVER CYNICISM

THE FIRST TIME I heard "AI in accounting," I didn't brush it off. I wanted to know more.

It was 2023, and I had signed up for the AICPA's Digital CPA Conference in Las Vegas. Most CPAs I knew were skeptical, and honestly, I couldn't blame them. We'd already been promised that desktop accounting would be a game changer, then that the cloud would set us free. Each phase brought improvements, but not transformation that was effective in building a work life balance.

Despite all the talk about efficiency, the reality was that most of us were still buried in manual reviews, late nights, and repetitive tasks that software never truly eliminated. Technology evolved, but the workload didn't seem to shrink in a way that freed us to focus on assisting our clients in making financial decisions that served them in the long run.

I wasn't seeing the kind of meaningful change that allowed me to step out of the day-to-day and into the role of true advisor. That is, until I attended this conference. I was overwhelmed with the number of vendors and inspirational stories. I was curious and excited about the coming changes. I was ready to learn and evolve.

THE SPARK IN LAS VEGAS

When I arrived at the Digital CPA Conference that December, the energy felt purposeful. It was focused and driven to inspire and change the minds of those in our profession. The sessions centered on technology, innovation, and how firms could evolve their business models to serve clients in new ways. For the first time, it felt like the profession was having a serious, practical conversation about change rather than just talking about the next upgrade or fix.

I sat in sessions about automation, data analytics, and client-advisory transformation, processing as quickly as the presenters could speak. With live demonstrations and firms putting this technology to use, this wasn't theory anymore; it was real application. The people on stage were firm owners and practitioners who had already begun integrating AI into their workflows, and the results they shared were tangible. They would share stories about how their data was more accurate, they had faster monthly closings, and they had reclaimed time for higher-value work. I was inspired to learn more about automation and align my business with this model.

Then came a demonstration that caught my attention completely. An AI-powered bookkeeping platform analyzed real transactions in seconds. It didn't just record them; it was learning through trial and error and reinforcement learning. It categorized expenses accurately, identified patterns, and flagged inconsistencies before they became problems.

Watching that demo, I didn't feel skeptical. I felt energized and excited. For the first time in years, I saw technology that could change the way I served clients. I was not worried about being replaced and was excited that the technology could provide accurate data entry and time savings.

That was the moment my curiosity turned into conviction. I knew I had to bring what I had learned back home and put it to work. I was energized and confident about the future of the profession.

TESTING AI IN CLOUD-BASED ACCOUNTING SYSTEM WORKFLOWS

When I got home, I started small. I didn't overhaul my entire system or roll out anything risky. Instead, I picked one client file in the cloud-based accounting system notorious for dropping every expense into "Miscellaneous." Normally, I'd spend hours reclassifying their accounts.

This time, I uploaded the transactions through the AI tool I'd seen at the conference. Within minutes, it had sorted everything perfectly. The categories were accurate: meals to meals, supplies to supplies, equipment purchases flagged for depreciation.

It was more than automation. The system *learned*. It recognized how the client spent money, how I categorized items in prior years, and how their business flowed through the seasons. I was collaborating with software. However, it was important to have human oversight to ensure the accuracy of automation.

That single test changed my entire workflow philosophy. I realized I could finally spend less time chasing down errors and more time giving clients insights. I could analyze what their margins meant, where they were overspending, and what trends might impact their next quarter.

THE SPREADSHEET AND PAPER BAG, REIMAGINED

There came a point when I had to make a hard but necessary decision. The unreconciled spreadsheets and the paper bag clients I had always tried to rescue could no longer continue that way. It wasn't out of frustration or a lack of compassion. It was about providing a better, more efficient way.

I created a client model built around partnership. One where I could truly help people move forward instead of constantly pulling them out of the same chaos each year. I knew some weren't ready, and that was okay. Sometimes, change doesn't fit the needs of all parties involved. I had come up with a plan, and I was going to test it across the board with my existing clients. A few clients decided this was not their direction. They had a different journey, and I wished them well.

To my satisfaction, even my longtime paper bag client embraced the change. He began using the secure system I set up for clients to scan and upload their documents directly. No more piles of receipts or time involved sorting.

WHAT AI REALLY GAVE ME: TIME AND BALANCE

AI didn't just save me hours. It allowed me to delve into my clients' books and talk with them more regularly about their business and how I could assist them in managing their business by providing data to them, which was concise and allowed them to make decisions that affected the growth of their business.

It wasn't about replacing what I did. It was about elevating it and giving more back to my clients in the form of information that they otherwise may not have seen or used in a productive manner. This allowed me to strategize and adjust items as needed to fit both their goals as well as put them in the best tax position that I could. What matters to me most in my practice is the relationships, the human connection, and giving back to my clients what they need to succeed with their businesses.

Software remained the backbone of my practice, but with AI supporting me and clients embracing new habits, my work felt purposeful instead of overwhelming.

For the first time, I saw what was possible when small firms stopped trying to do everything the old way and started using technology as a true partner.

CHAPTER 4

Why Small Firms Stand to Benefit the Most

I HAVE ALWAYS believed small firms have a secret weapon and that is relationships with their clients. Technology cannot replicate human relationships.

When you run a small firm, you know your clients' kids and families. You know their stresses and worries, as you are a sounding board of their everyday working life. You are a commandant and trusted advisor. This comes at a cost in small businesses, as you don't have the resources that larger firms have access to. Larger firms have multiple departments, such as audit, research, tax, etc. In a small firm, you generally have the owner, who wears six hats, and you maybe have one or two part-time employees.

If AI could reshape my small firm, what could it do for every small firm trying to remain relevant in a constantly changing world? The struggle to find talent and people interested in accounting is one of the biggest struggles for small firms. This is extremely relevant in areas that are rural and do not have the resources to draw talent from larger cities. I have been in business for nearly nineteen years. Throughout that time, I have always had part-time employees that assisted me primarily during tax season in the early years. As my business evolved, that would change to year-round part-time employees. Living in a mountain resort town already had its challenges for me and my business. However, I have trained over six employees in that period. This number may seem small, but training consumed valuable hours I didn't have to spare. The training was generally in the cloud-based accounting system and data entry. The cost to me for help in this area opened up hours for me to work on other areas of my practice, such as tax and tax law. Those hours are hidden costs that keep most small firms from growing and innovating.

When I stopped treating AI as a novelty and put it into motion to assist my firm with repetitive tasks, I saw immediate progress. I now use cloud-based accounting systems for all my clients. Routine tasks are automated, and guided workflows help new hires become productive much faster. With automation, I no longer spend time on repetitive tasks that small firms are forced to cover due to insufficient access to employees.

CASE STUDY

I was sitting in a conference room with a long-time friend and client. I met his new employee. She was wonderful and full of promise. She could definitely provide proper support for my client's internal needs. They divulged the issues they were facing with their current bookkeeping team and getting the construction draws ready to pay out and incorporate it with the current construction software they were using. I listened closely to each of them and the troubles they had been facing. I asked them to walk me through the process step-by-step. After hearing and understanding the setbacks they were facing, I determined they weren't using this new software properly and were essentially creating more work for themselves. The bookkeeping team was using spreadsheets to track items and then send the bills in one direction to be paid while still needing to enter the data in the construction software. I explained to them that we needed to revise the process and learn the software to better fit their needs and increase their efficiency. We all agreed that there were training modules in the software, and it would benefit them to put time aside to learn, as the end result would be much better for the whole team. The mood changed and there were smiles and promises that things would become more streamlined in the future, creating opportunities for other business needs. Both the employee and owner beamed with excitement. I was excited to share this journey with them.

Workflow Comparison

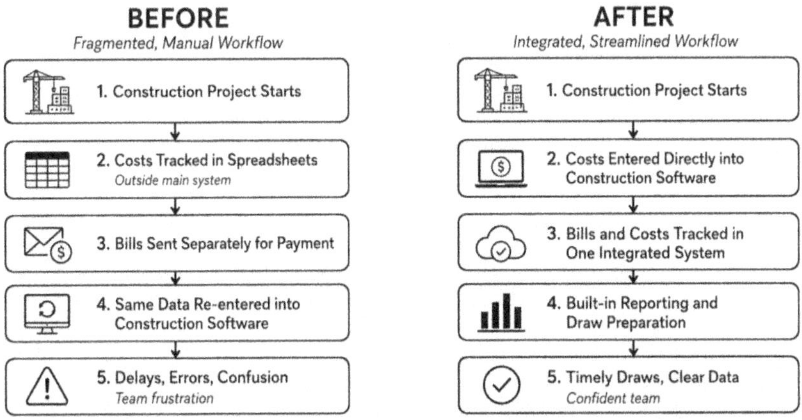

Before	After
Multiple tools	One integrated system
Manual spreadsheets	Direct system entry
Duplicate work	One-time input
Reactive fixes	Proactive insight
Team frustration	Team confidence

WHY SMALL FIRMS WIN

I realized small firms have trust, big firms have scale, and AI can bridge that gap. Large firms can throw people at the problem. However, they generally lack the intimacy of sitting in someone's home to assist them with their books or even just a lending ear. What I love about my small firm is my clients are not just a number. I dirt bike and camp with them. I eat dinner at their homes. I know their goals and dreams. And I care deeply. I believe in elevating community growth and supporting local entrepreneurs who contribute to a diverse and local economy. It is not just a paycheck for me; it is about offering a service and helping them obtain their version of the American Dream.

CHAPTER 5

Dos & Don'ts

TRANSITION TO THE SMART ADOPTION PLAYBOOK

IF YOU HAVE ever been to a Yoga class, they tell you each move should be initiated with intention. Starting small in your cloud-based accounting system means choosing a simple, predictable transaction to automate. It's foundational. It gives you the space to build confidence.

CHANGE MANAGEMENT WITH INTENTION

Change is never easy. It requires intention and awareness of who is impacted now and in the future. When you adjust a process, it doesn't just affect your internal workflow; it touches customers, subcontractors, and anyone who depends on your systems. You need to be mindful of how the change affects them. That is why communication, training, and patience are as important as technology itself.

Before adopting AI in my practice, I communicated what was changing and why. Be sure your clients, team members, and outside partners are factored into the process. Make sure your team is bought into the plan.

DO #1: START SMALL AND SOLVE ONE PROBLEM

Identify a problem and look for a resolution to this problem. Do not try to solve everything at once. Start with a small interaction. Choose one client with one issue.

I had a client whom I took on in the middle of the year in 2025. Their books had not been completed for 2024, and the taxes were not complete for that fiscal year. I'll be honest; I felt overwhelmed. I knew I needed to take the right action rather than worrying about the results. I needed to act intentionally rather than get lost worrying about the outcome.

How could I enter a year's worth of data efficiently and effectively without spending days completing this task? I feel that data entry is a boring task; however, it is essential that the books are complete before a tax return can be completed. With that identified, I started reviewing the unposted entries, and I looked for consistency and repetition. I created my first rule, which was an entry for accounting fees that were the same amount each month and posted on the same date each month. Eighteen transactions followed the parameters I set, and I chose to automatically enter that data. With thousands of uncategorized entries, we eliminated eighteen right there!

I tested the rule, and that "aha" moment struck. That small success gave me confidence to build the next rule, then another, following the same logic: consistency and repetition. Rinse and repeat.

By focusing on action and process, not the end result, I built momentum. Thousands of uncategorized transactions slowly turned into organized data and clean books. We found the finish line and the result we were looking for. Smart adoption is seeing the small successes and letting each win fuel the next.

Encouraged, I decided I needed to delve into some training and understanding to set up more complex rules. I was looking for patterns. Recurring vendor payments, fuel charges from specific gas stations, even reoccurring bills. I was essentially teaching QBO to understand my logic, my workflow, and a set of standards.

This process did not only save me time, but I was also able to reclaim my mental space. I felt confident opening this set of books with the proper set of rules in place. I could trust the system. However, I also acknowledged that a system may make errors, so you must regularly check the system to be sure it is accurate.

If you are drowning in misclassification of transactions, take it from me: Don't underestimate the power of a well-crafted rule. Look at it as a lifeline, not a feature.

DO #2: CHOOSE TOOLS THAT WORK INSIDE YOUR SYSTEM

When adopting AI or any automation tool, compatibility matters more than capability. The best solution isn't the one with all the promises and features; it is the one that integrates seamlessly with how you already work.

When redesigning workflows, you must cater to the client's needs. Incorporate tools that are useful and create time saving for their company and industry. Don't overload the tech stack. The aim is to reduce costs ultimately, but the bigger impact is freeing up time. If you can improve customer satisfaction, competitive differentiation, profit and growth while also cultivating a culture that doesn't work people to the bone, you're not just redesigning workflows; you are reshaping the organization for long-term success.

AI and robots won't steal your job, but someone using AI will. Large companies are already making transitions to implement changes to their core operations. For small firms to stay relevant and up to speed with their competitors, it is highly advised they move out of their comfort zone. I know small firms find themselves overwhelmed with the choices. You don't want to be outpaced in this changing market, as small firms do not have access to as many resources as large firms. Let's face it: Everyone seems to be developing a product that offers time savings and the answer to the pain points of small businesses. However, you want to be sure to adopt AI strategically with a vision that fits your business and won't outpace you before you even implement it.

Think of AI as a tool rather than a threat. Like any tool, its value depends on who is using it: people who continue to educate themselves, embrace experimentation, and build workflows that combine results of machine learning and human creativity.

DO #3: ALIGN PEOPLE WITH THE PROCESS

Technology can deliver meaningful results only when people are part of the journey.

As a business owner, you must recognize that change extends beyond you. It touches everyone connected to the system, from internal staff to subcontractors and clients. Before rolling out new processes, set your expectations upfront and communicate the benefits to all involved.

I was working with a contractor client as an advisor and support system as their business grew. The business grew quickly, and they were working with a bookkeeper who integrated a cloud-based accounting system, spreadsheets, and a bill pay solution. Then, the contractor introduced a technology solution that streamlined project workflows from planning to completion. The introduction of this new solution did not have a plan in place. Putting the cart before the horse created bottlenecks, late payments, and other issues. The bookkeepers did their best to work this new system into the existing system, but it turned out to be a square peg trying to fit into a round hole. We addressed the issue and realized that we needed a clear plan in place to transition to the software that benefited the contractor and his growing business. The following points were communicated to all involved: why the change was necessary, who was affected, what was expected, and how they would be supported. The team came up with a plan that everyone was committed to. The plan had intention, compliance, and cooperation. There was a lot of buzz and excitement as we moved forward on this journey of introducing AI and a system that promised efficiency and time savings.

DON'T CHASE SHINY OBJECTS

As you transition to using AI in your current systems, you will undoubtedly be provided with plenty of demos and solutions that promise to provide time savings. However, be careful not to fall for the first pretty demo with colorful dashboards and sophisticated interfaces. You must consider how this solution will fit into your current workflows and processes. You don't want to recreate your workflows or add additional steps or extra time to review. Ask yourself: *Does it solve any of the root problems or pain points of my current business?*

Be sure to focus on what needs solving to ensure you get back more time but make sure that it also doesn't disrupt your core operations. It should integrate with your current system. If it requires you to reinvent your client's process while promising to save time, but instead absorbs all your time, it is not the solution you are looking for. It is merely a distraction.

PITFALLS TO AVOID (DON'TS)

I attended a conference in Las Vegas a year after ChatGPT came out. The buzz was alive and well in the AI world. However, many vendors were trying to get ahead of the curve as the next promising solution. I met with a vendor at a networking event. His idea was to find common matches within data entry for bookkeeping to match the data without having to enter each item. I was already using a cloud-based accounting system with some level of automation. Although in 2023 it was not quite as advanced as today, I almost made a transition to the software I was introduced to at the conference without proper oversight.

What I learned quickly is that the tool was sleek and had a lot of future forward thinking. I thought for sure it could save me hours of work. As I started delving into it, I realized it wasn't that the technology was bad; it just didn't fit into the current processes. Was I willing to rework my client's current workflow and add steps to make something work that I had no experience with? I put on the brakes and looked from the outside in. I realized that I had to slow down on implementing something too quickly.

Sometimes success is the step you don't take. I realized that adopting AI isn't just how to do it; it's also about building the right guardrails and security measures to avoid pitfalls. Success requires diligence, pace, and risk control before innovation can truly take off. You cannot solve the problem in one sitting. It requires patience, safeguards, and a commitment to meaningful progress.

DON'T NEGLECT CYBERSECURITY

As accountants, we are held to a higher standard. As a CPA, AICPA requires all professionals to safeguard client data. We must make a reasonable effort to protect taxpayers' information. This is no different with using AI, and all small business professionals should adhere to security standards and encryption.

Security in a small business should not be overlooked. Just think of a data breach and the cost to a small business. It could be catastrophic.

AI may help us work faster, but our responsibility to protect client information never changes. Before I implemented my new system, I made sure it met the same level of confidentiality I uphold in every part of my practice. It had to be encrypted. It had to offer secure transmission and storage. And above all, it had to be aligned with established accounting ethics and professional standards. It is our job as humans to verify and question the data AI generates, as there are still many kinks to be worked out.

DON'T FORGET CLIENT TRUST

I remember the first time a client said, "So… is the computer doing my taxes now?" I needed to reassure them I was still part of the process. Technology can do repetitive work, but it cannot replace human connections and expertise. As an accountant, I am a trusted advisor for a reason. People don't come to us because we are fast. They don't come to us because we are efficient. We bring expertise and experience to the relationship.

Client relations are not transactional; they are relational. They are built slowly like the roots of a tree. Each conversation, each piece of advice and expertise paves the way for the relationship that is built. Over time, those roots grow deeper and withstand uncertainty, change, and disruption. The software can crunch numbers, but it doesn't understand the story behind those numbers. A computer cannot relate to the worries and stresses of a business owner. And it certainly can't have compassion during difficult times. As an advisor, your clients need trust and guidance. Technology cannot replace the human connection in all of this.

DON'T FORGET THE WHY

When I first started using automation and AI in my practice, it was easy to be excited about the accuracy and efficiency of the new process. However, it was just a tool. It's not the purpose.

Communicate clearly to your clients the "why" in the use of automation. When I took over a large client, I explained I started using the "rules" feature in QBO to automate data entry and provide consistency and accuracy in the books. Human oversight in the workflow process ultimately provided an accurate set of books, something the client did not have in the past. Seeing the results ultimately proved to be a great success, and the client was happy with the outcome.

Keeping the "why" front and center ensures that AI strengthens the mission rather than becomes the mission.

Why do you need to adapt? You have heard the term, "Work smarter, not harder." Well, I have always been an advocate of this idea. What gets to me is when people state that you are not working as hard due to using technology. I take offense to that. My goal has always been to offer my clients a better service. I operate with integrity and honesty, and that is what most clients look for in an accountant. If you are serving your clients and providing them with a top-notch service, what does it matter how you achieve that goal?

CHAPTER 6

The World is Big and Then There is Main Street

AT FIRST GLANCE, the world feels enormous. But look closer. Really look and you will start to see the same patterns repeating themselves in every corner of middle America. A property management company in Colorado, a tech startup in Austin, and a nonprofit stretching every dollar to survive another fiscal year. On paper, they couldn't be more different. Spread across a sprawling map, they appear unrelated. Yet in reality, they are all doing the same things humans do by putting one foot in front of the other. You hear the same concerns spoken in different voices. The same bottlenecks are described using different jargon. The same stress disguised as "just part of the job." And always, the same fear of letting go of the systems that work but feel safe simply because they are known. Somewhere between a client call and a casual conversation, you realize you have heard this story before.

It happened to me on a ski lift in Breckenridge. High alpine air, a bluebird sky day, strangers sharing a chair because that is how mountain towns work. A tourist marveled at how amazing and beautiful it is, saying they wished they could live here and experience this wonderland every day. I replied with, "I do live here." I made the decision young, came to work, and stayed long enough to build a new career." No titles, no credentials, just helmets, goggles, and idle talk.

One person on the lift worked in the hospitality industry. Another was a consultant in Denver. Someone on the lift joked they'd spent more time on calls and responding to emails than skiing. By the time we reached the top, the pattern was established. Different industries, different lives, yet the same friction exists across industries with manual processes and late nights spent managing work that no longer adds value. At that moment, the work didn't feel big at all. It felt compressed into a single chairlift conversation.

Accounting lives in that intersection. Every ledger is a meeting point. Every transaction is a quiet handshake between people who may never meet. Long before AI entered the conversation, accounting was already documenting how closely our decisions and outcomes intertwine.

AI simply revealed how small the world really is. What once felt like a massive, unmanageable city, too many spreadsheets, too many systems, too many rules, suddenly showed its patterns. The same inefficiencies repeat across industries. The same resistance appears under different titles. Not because people refuse to change, but because they haven't yet seen the map.

This is where the divide begins. Some professionals recognize the intersections. They see how a conversation on a ski lift mirrors one happening in a boardroom three days later. They upskill not to chase technology, but to remain relevant in a world where problems repeat faster than excuses.

Others are content to stay put. They grind away, convinced their situation is uniquely complex. They call the city overwhelming, unaware that what feels like size is actually distance. Step back from the tools so you can see the bigger picture and move forward with clarity. You need the vision and space to make strategic progress.

AI doesn't replace judgment; it demands it. It turns accountants from record keepers into translators and people who understand how numbers connect lives, industries, and decisions across time and geography. It doesn't remove the human element; it magnifies it.

The world is vast, but the patterns are familiar. And once you've seen them, once you've heard from the echo on a chair lift in Breckenridge to a conference room back home, you can't pretend the city is too big to navigate anymore.

CHAPTER 7

Leveling the Field

THE FIRST YEAR I used AI during tax season, I was blown away. I started with automation of the engagement letters. With my new business model, I required monthly contracts for my business clients for books and payroll, which minimized chasing down a year's worth of items in a short period of time. It also allowed me to set up the automation for the data entry piece throughout the year for the bookkeeping. As a result, I did not spend hours fixing books and late nights preparing the tax return.

This is how small firms fight back. We are not concerned about becoming the next Big Four. When you have a clear picture of the financial position, you are able to step back and look at the numbers to provide more depth for the business. For example, if you have a slow year in earnings, where can you cut overhead spending? The data inevitably reveals the answers to these questions, and you can pivot and make necessary adjustments in spending. It's about being relevant and offering value by delivering insights that rival or even outpace bigger competitors.

CASE IN POINT: CONTRACTOR CLIENT

One of my clients runs a contractor service in our community. I had known him for years. My husband and he talked, and he was looking for a change. We spoke in May and by July, we were working together. What I uncovered is there were a lot of items unresolved in the prior year, and the taxes for that year had not been filed yet. I learned that his margins were a bit tight, and he had been running the business with no financial oversight from inception. He did not have the budget for "CFO to hire" type of service. His prior accountant charged him for compliance services such as bookkeeping and tax, but very little work was done.

I needed to act fast and efficiently, as time was of the essence. The extension deadline was closing in less than six weeks to complete the return. AI was my resolution to his problem. I implemented this immediately, got him online with payroll, and had over a year and a half of books completed in a few days. If I had to go back to my desktop warrior days, this job would have taken months. Now that he is back on track with compliance, I have time to assist him with more meaningful financial data and assist him with decisions and cash flow related items. AI didn't just make me faster; it made me more valuable to my clients.

AI ISN'T MAGIC; IT'S LEVERAGE.

I had a vendor meeting the other day, and I likely had twenty years in age on the two people I met with on Zoom. They were passionate about a new product their company launched and were sharing with me the benefits of the product. We talked about the use of spreadsheets and how sometimes they create bottlenecks in the workflows and create a confusing process, leading people to believe they cannot effectively automate. We need to get out of the spreadsheets and utilize the vast majority of products that provide tools to increase efficiencies with workflow, financial reporting, dashboards, etc.

Essentially, my client would be getting an HR person representing his small business for a fraction of the cost of hiring HR personnel. The cost benefit was staggering. Small businesses have to be in compliance with labor laws just like a larger company. However, often they don' t know where to go to get answers to important questions. This solution was the answer. They could ask the questions they needed by signing up for this HR product solution offered through their third-party payroll.

Building relationships between my clients and vendors has allowed me to offer services to my clients that I didn't have time for before. Not only did this help me build a practice with a steady source of income, but it strengthened my relationship with my clients. Especially with the added support and efficiency that AI brings.

CHAPTER 8

Work, Family, and Freedom

THE FIRST FREE EVENING

I WILL NEVER forget it. It was February, the heart of tax season. Normally, I would be surviving on quick snacks and caffeine, telling my family, "I will make it up to you after April 15."

My friends asked our family to join them on a hut trip outside of Aspen in February. What this meant was two nights with absolutely no cell service or internet. It was a quiet cabin on top of the mountain with clear skies, with the best view of the skyline and vibrant bright stars. In previous years, I would have laughed as if that idea was unheard of.

With a bit of anxiety, I booked the trip through the hut trip system and thought, *I can manage two nights away. I am not a surgeon; no one will die on my watch.* AI had revamped my workload; this year was different. I had streamlined a lot of my work prior to year-end and had set myself up to be away. I had advised clients I would not be available, and it was not an issue at all.

My family and I made our way up the mountain on skis for about six miles to the cabin with our friends. No internet, no computers, and no way of communicating. I sat under the stars and thought, *this is freedom and pure solace, this is the balance of life I need.* I came back refreshed and, in my opinion, a better advisor to my clients than previous years, as I was fresh and focused from a small break that many accountants don't allow themselves during "busy season."

WHAT CLIENTS REALLY WANT

It wasn't just me. My clients felt it, too. A painter I have worked with for years told me, "The best thing I ever did was hire an accountant to do the work for me. It gives me peace of mind that my books are done right as well as my taxes." He cared about his free time and preferred to focus on what he is good at: painting and managing jobs.

That is the heart of it. Small business owners don't dream about "automation" or "machine learning." They dream about time with their family, recreating and enjoying life, vacations without worrying, and the ability to step away from their business without it falling apart.

Peace of mind and financial security are what most small business owners want. By eliminating transactional monotony and using automation, I could act as their advisor. I prefer being involved in the process and advising rather than putting out fires once a year. This allowed me to provide a service that clients needed, whether they knew it or not.

THE FAMILY LEDGER

That realization led me to think differently about my work. So much accounting is about ledgers: assets, liabilities, and equity. But there is another ledger we don't talk about enough: family.

On one side are the hours we give to our work. On the other are the moments we give to the people we love. For years, this equation was unbalanced. My clients were unbalanced as well.

AI didn't magically fix everything. It created the efficiency I needed to provide more meaningful services to my clients. It allowed me to operate with intention rather than urgency.

And in doing so, it helped me restore something far more valuable than time. It helped me restore presence.

FREEDOM ISN'T JUST MONEY

Many Americans equate freedom with income. If I work harder, bill more hours, and grow my client base, I will "earn" the life I crave. But the truth is, this earns exhaustion and burnout.

I got into accounting for freedom, not just my own, but for the small business owners who feel overwhelmed by the financial side of running a business.

I chose this work because I was good with numbers, and I loved solving problems. Often, I was not able to problem solve, as I was spending my time on transactional and compliance accounting. Over time, the long nights, the constant deadlines, and the endless software cleanups made me forget what freedom felt like. AI became the latest chapter in that pursuit.

That changed the year AI entered my practice. No one cared how the mundane repetitive tasks were completed. If I could deliver data that was meaningful, such as timely tax planning and review of trends in the books, I could advise my clients to make decisions that impacted them financially. We could be proactive with reducing tax liability and make re-investment decisions in the business with complete and timely data.

CHAPTER 9

Leadership, Culture, and Training

WORK SMARTER, NOT HARDER

WORK SMARTER, NOT harder. A term many of us have heard and often don't put into action. Like each generation of humans, we evolve and throughout history, we have been shown how tools or systems were used to improve efficiencies. Henry Ford's assembly line created a level of standardization, division of labor, and affordability. With AI, we can revolutionize our modern-day business to utilize technology to increase efficiencies on mundane repetitive tasks similar to the assembly line. The technology is more dynamic, but the premise is essentially the same.

Technology alone does not guarantee success. The true differentiation lies in leadership, culture, and training. Leaders must set the tone, not only by adopting AI but also by shaping a vision of how it enhances human work. Just as Ford's assembly line required managers to rethink workflows and encourage workers to embrace new methods, today's leaders must champion AI as a partner in progress.

The leadership is there to direct and define the culture of the organization. If you don't have a culture that encourages curiosity and exploration, you may find that your organization is not fit to implement AI just yet. There needs to be a standard of communication and culture to connect any new systems.

Culture is the soil in which innovation grows. A fearful culture will likely resist change, but a culture of curiosity, collaboration, and adaptability thrives. It is no surprise that the accounting industry has been notoriously equated with grueling long hours and what seems to be never ending deadlines. It starts with rethinking your business model. Making a cultural shift away from the old and into the new is as important as technology. We are not talking about just installing some software and *voila'*, the change is complete. It's about cultivating a mindset where employees see technology as an ally. Empower your employees to experiment with AI, to learn and evaluate. This enhances the buy-in if they are involved in the process and does not make them feel like they are being replaced.

Training your employees is essential in AI transformation. Today's workforce must learn the skills to navigate the use of AI. Training must be made a priority and not a one-time event. It should be continuous, collaborative, and adaptive. Transformation will not happen overnight. It is important to include training goals in performance evaluations and possibly other incentives. Give staff the opportunity and time to explore and experiment with technology without the pressure to keep up with billable hours or other engagement budgets. With younger generations entering the workforce, plan to nurture in-house resources and create a group of knowledgeable technology users.

Leadership sets the direction, culture fuels the journey, and training equips the workforce. The transformation should not be seen as just another tool, but a transformative force that allows small businesses to truly work smarter, not harder. Businesses that embrace this triad will be future-ready and will thrive in this new environment.

FUTURE READY AND REDEFINING THE DREAM

When I think about the American Dream now, it has changed from the corner office to something much simpler. It is regaining time to commit to the things that matter to me. That picture is different for everyone. For me, it allows me to spend time with my family, recreating and exercising. It is taking the afternoon to go to the ski area and watch my kids' race. For my client, it could be a road trip with their young daughter to see the Grand Canyon for the first time.

The Dream isn't about working yourself to death for success and a nice house. More is not better. Thinking big and thinking more is better are two different notions. It's about building something sustainable enough that you can live while you build it. Simplicity can be a strategy and a solution.

I am not threatened by AI or technology. I believe we can utilize it to harmoniously work in conjunction with small businesses to provide more balance.

The American Dream to me is a combination of hope, inspiration, and innovation. What a more cohesive and less stressful tomorrow can bring. It is not a white picket fence, and a three-bedroom house with two and a half kids, and a dog. It is the power of change. How we embrace and learn with technology and growth is who we will be tomorrow. I desire to stay relevant and continue to harbor a culture of learning and curiosity into tomorrow's innovations. I want my clients and other small businesses to regain time and relevance in their world, whether that be family time, recreation, learning, travel, and so much more.

PIVOT WITH PURPOSE

The foundation to success is identifying key factors (pain points) and building a solution around these to become innovative and relevant. When you are wearing six different hats as a business owner, you want someone to tell you what is going to work for you without trial and error. Unfortunately, it is too personal and must be approached with diligence and caution. Look at challenges as an opportunity, not a threat. If you don't do it, someone else likely will.

AI brings tremendous opportunity, but it also comes with challenges. Like any new system, implementation matters as much as the tool itself.

Early in my transition to AI-assisted workflows, I made a mistake that taught me an important lesson.

We transitioned a client to a new software that was integrated with an internal bill pay option. We were not ready at that time to transition all the vendor data into the new system. Therefore, we stuck with the external bill paying system, which required manual entry. However, we moved too quickly and did not build a proper implementation plan. We lacked documentation on required steps in the workflow. Within a few weeks, we noticed multiple bills had been paid twice.

It wasn't a catastrophic failure, but it was serious enough to demand immediate attention. The owner and I gathered after I audited the details of the over payment. We discovered the problem was due to the process, not technology.

Our Standard Operating Procedure (SOP) had gaps. The intake of invoices was unclear, and vendors emailed to various emails. Certain transactions were being pushed through multiple channels without clear verification. Automation had simply accelerated a flawed workflow.

We rebuilt the system. We documented the steps and added verification points. We clarified responsibilities and created a clear audit trail for payments. The result was far better than the original process.

The lesson here is that failure, when handled correctly, becomes instruction. You must move forward with intention not speed. AI works best when you start small, document clearly, and give the team time to learn. When you pivot with purpose, even mistakes become part of building a better stronger system.

STAYING RELEVANT IN A DISRUPTIVE WORLD

Many people see AI as disruptive change. There is a volatile balance you must work toward in the ever-changing world of disruption. There is not a one size fits all approach to implementing automation.

I love telling my kids who are Gen Z about the rotary phone in the kitchen and that my first cell phone was a Nokia, and I explain how long it took to text a message. I look at the fact that the iPhone will be twenty years old in 2027. I started my business the same year the Apple iPhone came out. In that time, the workflow and processes in my business have changed tremendously, from the day I opened my doors. If you thought the iPhone was going to fail when it came out, you likely don't like the hype around AI and say that robots are going to take over people's jobs. Yet Nokia became obsolete overnight. We are in a state of disruptive change. I was inspired by the work of Pascal Finette in his book, "Disrupt Disruption: How to Decode the Future, Disrupt Your Industry, and Transform Your Business.

Being in business nowadays is almost analogous with playing the stock market. You have to look ahead, learn and understand the trends, and where and when the next best tool is going to be introduced. Can this tool assist you, project you into future success, and help you remain relevant? Are you able to identify the tools and skills you need to continue to upskill and remain competitive? Stay ahead of the curve. Evaluate your processes and identify technology that will alleviate repetitive tasks. It likely won't be one level of technology. Remain curious and inquisitive, explore options, and try them in small chunks. Think about how the customer experience will play out and how to serve them best. You are not going to check the boxes on client happiness across the board but if you shoot for a majority buy-in, then you are making strides as you move forward. There is not a playbook on implementation. You need to identify the areas in your business that can benefit from transformation. Identify your specific circumstances and define your culture to lead you through this journey.

When I look back on my grandfather's career and recall the long hours, the stress of getting it right the first time without the technology we have today, I don't see failure. I see dedication and care for his clients. But I also see a version of success that demanded too much from the people who carried it. You have the opportunity to honor the legacy without repeating it. You can build a business that serves others and leaves room for your life beyond work. Let this be your permission to choose progress over exhaustion, intention over urgency, and balance over burn out. The tools are finally here to support the American Dream before us. Are you *in* to upskill yourself and your business or are you *out*?

www.ingramcontent.com/pod-product-compliance
Lightning Source LLC
LaVergne TN
LVHW022028200926
848481LV00007B/2596

* 9 7 9 8 9 0 3 8 9 0 1 1 8 *